Vril
The Power
of the
Coming Race
6,908 words
used

By Gregory Zorzos

Gregory Zorzos, a native Hellene, was born in Kallithea, Athens in Greece (Hellas) at 1958. Author and his research work have been distinguished by a lot of official organizations, and Ministries, in Greece and all over the world. The author has wrote and published more than 3,500,000 works (books, board games, DVDs, CD-Roms, DVD-Roms, audio CDs, MP3s, E-books, E-pubs, MP4s etc) about ancient and modern history in the fields of economics, technical, board games, martial arts, software, love affairs, feasibilities studies, research, case studies, learning languages, logodynamics, inner research etc. Many awards and credits around the world. As a reporter, from his teens, the author has written many articles in many newspapers, magazines etc and was editor in chief in some of them. Researches have been approved or accepted from the Ministry of Education, Ministry of Culture, Hellenic Army, Ministry of Foreign Affairs, Group Unesco Piraeus and Islands, SAE, etc. Works have been register in Copyright Offices in Greece, USA and Canada.

Vril
The Power of the Coming Race
6,908 words used

Most common word: the (3441 times)

First char cnt/percent - total char counter (cnt/percent)

	First char cnt/percent	total char counter (cnt/percent)
A:	565 (8.2%)	3632 (7.2%)
B:	293 (4.2%)	739 (1.5%)
C:	663 (9.6%)	2059 (4.1%)
D:	470 (6.8%)	2316 (4.6%)
E:	352 (5.1%)	6547 (13.0%)
F:	327 (4.7%)	797 (1.6%)
G:	209 (3.0%)	1368 (2.7%)
H:	226 (3.3%)	1073 (2.1%)
I:	351 (5.1%)	4224 (8.4%)
J:	32 (0.5%)	72 (0.1%)
K:	34 (0.5%)	273 (0.5%)
L:	224 (3.2%)	2581 (5.1%)
M:	310 (4.5%)	1354 (2.7%)
N:	119 (1.7%)	3763 (7.5%)
O:	158 (2.3%)	2954 (5.9%)
P:	546 (7.9%)	1406 (2.8%)
Q:	24 (0.3%)	87 (0.2%)
R:	406 (5.9%)	3644 (7.2%)
S:	753 (10.9%)	4013 (8.0%)
T:	314 (4.5%)	3597 (7.1%)
U:	136 (2.0%)	1707 (3.4%)
V:	122 (1.8%)	708 (1.4%)
W:	216 (3.1%)	469 (0.9%)
X:	20 (0.3%)	193 (0.4%)
Y:	28 (0.4%)	844 (1.7%)
Z:	10 (0.1%)	46 (0.1%)

WordLen: counter / percent
1: 15 (0.2%)
2: 54 (0.8%)
3: 210 (3.0%)
4: 585 (8.5%)
5: 824 (11.9%)
6: 1049 (15.2%)
7: 1085 (15.7%)
8: 1008 (14.6%)
9: 801 (11.6%)
10: 560 (8.1%)
11: 365 (5.3%)
12: 194 (2.8%)
13: 96 (1.4%)
14: 42 (0.6%)
15: 15 (0.2%)
16: 2 (0.0%)
17: 1 (0.0%)
18: 1 (0.0%)
19: 0 (0.0%)
20: 1 (0.0%)

Vril
The Power of the Coming Race
6,908 words used

a
abandon
abashed
abbreviated
aberration
abhorrent
abilities
ablative
able
abnormal
abode
abodes
abolish
abominable
aboriginal
abound
abounded
abounds
about
above
abreast
abroad
abrogate
abrupt
abruptly
abruptness
absence
absolute
absolutely
absorbed

absorbing
abstain
abstinence
abstract
abstracted
abstraction
abstruse
absurd
abundant
abundantly
abuse
abyss
abysses
ac
acanthus
accent
accents
accept
acceptable
accepted
accident
accompanied
accompanies
accompany
accomplish
accomplished
accomplishments
accorded
according
accordingly

accosted	adding
accosting	additions
account	address
accounted	addressed
accounts	addresses
accurate	addressing
accurately	adequate
accustom	adherence
accustomed	adherents
achieve	adhesiveness
achieved	adjoining
achievement	adjuration
achievements	adjure
acknowledge	administered
acknowledged	administration
acquaintance	administrator
acquainted	administrators
acquired	admiration
acquirements	admire
acquiring	admired
acquisition	admit
acquitted	admitted
across	admitting
act	admixture
acted	adolescence
acting	adopt
action	adopted
active	adopting
actively	adorable
acts	adorn
actual	adorning
actually	adult
acute	adulterate
acutely	adulterer
adaptation	adults
adapted	advance
add	advanced
added	advancement

advances

advantage

advent

adventure

adventures

adventurous

advice

advise

advocating

aerial

afar

affairs

affected

affecting

affection

affectionate

affections

affects

affianced

affinity

afflicted

affliction

afford

afforded

afraid

afresh

after

afterwards

again

against

agassiz

age

agencies

agency

agent

ages

agglutinative

aggrandisement

aggravated

aggravation

aggregate

aggressions

aggressive

aggrieved

aghast

agitated

aglauran

ago

agree

agreeable

agreeably

agreed

agreement

agreements

agricultural

agriculture

ah

aid

aim

aims

air

airs

akin

alarm

alarmed

alas

alcohol

alcoholic

alert

alighted

alighting

alike

aliment

alive

all

alleged

allegorical	amazes
alliance	amazingly
allied	ambition
allies	amenities
alligator	amenity
allotments	america
allotted	american
allow	amiable
allowable	amicable
allowance	amid
allowances	amidst
allowed	among
allowing	amongst
allows	amorous
allure	amount
allured	amounting
almighty	amour
almost	ample
aloe	ampler
aloft	
alone	amuse
along	amused
aloud	amusement
alphabet	amusements
alpine	amuses
already	amusing
also	an
alterations	ana
altered	analogical
altogether	analogous
always	analogy
am	analysed
amalgamate	analyses
amateurs	anam
amativeness	ananda
amatory	anatomical
amaze	ancestors
amazed	ancient

anciently
and
angel
angelical
angle
angles
anglo
angrily
angry
angular
animal
animals
animate
animated
animosities
anly
annals
annihilated
annihilating
annihilation
announcements
annul
annulled
ano
anoi
another
ansa
answer
answered
answering
answers
antagonism
antagonistic
antecedents
antediluvian
antelope
anterior
anticipate

anticipated
antics
antiquated
antiquities
antiquity
anxiety
anxious
any
anything
apart
apartment
apartments
ape
apertures
apex
aph
aphorism
appalling
appals
apparatus
apparent
apparently
appealing
appear
appearance

appeared
appears
appertained
appetite
application
applications
applied
apply
appoint
appointed
appreciate
appreciation

apprehend

apprehended

apprehensions

approach

approached

approaches

approaching

approbation

appropriate

appropriated

appropriately

approval

approve

approximate

appurtenances

apropos

arabian

araucaria

arbitrary

arbitration

arch

arched

architectural

architecture

archives

ardent

ardently

ardour

are

area

argue

argued

argues

arguing

argument

arguments

arise

arising

aristocracy

aristocratic

aristotle

arm

armed

armies

armour

arms

army

arn

arna

arose

around

aroused

arouses

arranged

arrangement

arrested

arrival

arrive

arrived

arriving

arrogance

arrogate

arrows

art

arterial

artful

articles

artificial

artificially

artillery

artists

arts

aryan

as

ascend

ascendancy

ascended
ascending
ascent
ascertain
ascertaining
ascertainment
ascribed
ascribes
ashamed
ashes
ashore
aside
ask
asked
asking
asleep
aspect
aspirations
aspire
aspiring
assailed
assailing
assemblage
assemble
assembled
assemblies
assembly
assent
assert
asserted
asserters
asserting
assertor
assigned
assimilate
assist
assistant
associations

assume
assumed
assumption
assurance
assured
astonished
astonishing
astonishment
asunder
at
ata
ate
athens
atmosphere
atmospheric
attach
attached
attachment
attack
attacks
attain
attained
attaining
attainment
attains
attempt
attempted
attempting
attempts
attend
attendance
attended
attending
attends
attention
attentions
attest
attire

attired
attract
attraction
attractions
attracts
attribute
attributes
aub
auburn
audacious
audaciously
audience
aught
augmenting
augustus
aur
author
authorities
authority
authors
autocracy
automata
automaton
auxiliaries
auxiliary
avail
available
avarice
average
averse
averted
aviary
avidity
avocation
avocations
avoid
avoidance
avoided

awaited
awake
awakened
awakens
awarded
aware
away
awe
awed
awful
awkwardness
awoke
ay
babies
back
background
backgrounds
bad
bade
baffled
balconies
balcony
ball
ballet
balloon
balloons
balls
banal
band
bands
banish
bank
banks
banquet
barbarian
barbarians
barbaric
barbarism

barbarous	bees
barren	befall
base	befallen
based	befell
bashful	before
bashfully	beg
baskets	began
basks	begged
bath	beginning
bathing	begun
baths	behalf
batrachian	beheld
battle	behind
bber	behold
be	beholder
bear	being
beardless	beings
bearer	belief
bearing	believe
bearings	believed
beast	believing
beasts	belly
beatified	belong
beauteous	belonged
beautiful	belonging
beautify	belongs
beauty	beloved
became	below
because	bended
beck	bending
become	beneath
becomes	beneficent
becoming	benefit
bed	benevolence
beds	benevolent
bedside	benevolently
beecher	benighted
been	benignant

benignity
bent
bequeathed
berlin
beside
besides
best
bestow
bestowal
bestowed
betokened
betray
betraying
betrothed
better
between
beverage
bewildered
bewildering
bewilderment
beyond
bias
bigger
bills
bind
binding
biology
bird
birds
birth
bit
bitter
bitterly
bitterness
black
blackened
bladder
bladders

blade
blame
blank
blasted

blasts
blazed
bless
blessed
blessing
blessings
blind
bliss
blissful
block
blocks
blow
blows
blue
bluish
blundering
blushed
blushing
board
boasted
boastful
boasting
boat
boats
bodh
bodies
bodily
body
bold
boldly
boldness
bond
bone

bones
book
books
bootmaker
border
bordered
bordering
borders
born
borne
borrow
borrowed
bosh
boston
both
bottom
bought
bound
boundaries
boundary
bounding
bowed
bowels
bower
bows
boy
boyhood
boys
bra
braced
brachycephalic
brain
brained
brains
branched
branches
branching
brandy

brave
braving
breach
breadth
breaking
breast
breasts
breath
breathe
breathed
breathing
bred
breech
breed
breeders
breeding
brevity
bridal
bride
brief
briefer
briefly
bright
brighten
brightened
brightly
brilliant
brilliantly
bring
bringing
bristling
broached
broad
broadest
broadly
broadway
broken
bronze

brooding	butterfly
brother	buy
brothers	by
brought	c
brow	cage
brown	cages
brows	calamities
bruises	calamity
brute	
bubbling	calculated
bud	call
budh	called
build	calm
building	calmer
buildings	calmly
builds	calumnies
bulk	calumny
bull	came
bullfinches	camel
bulwer	can
buoy	cane
buoyed	cankered
burden	cannon
burial	cannons
buried	cannot
burned	canst
burning	canvas
burns	canvassed
burnt	capable
burst	capacities
bush	capacity
bushes	capillary
busied	capital
business	capitals
busy	caprice
but	captivate
butchered	captured
butler	care

carefully
careless
carelessly
cares
caress
caressing
caricature
carnivorous
carpeted
carpeting
carriage
carried
carrying
case
casement
cases
cast
casting
castles
catapults
catch
catching
category
caught
causality
cause
caused
causes
caution
cautious
cautiously
cave
cavern
cavernous
caverns
cavilled
cavities
ceased

ceases
ceiling
celestial
celtic
cemetery
censers
central
centre
centuries
century
cerebral
cerement
ceremonies
ceremony
certain
certainly
certainty
cessation
chaffed
chamber
chambers
chance
chances
change
changeability
changed
changeful
changes
changing
channels
chant
chanting
chaos
chaperons
chapter
character
characterise
characterised

characterises	chins
characteristic	chivalrous
characteristics	choice
characters	choicest
charge	choked
charged	choose
charlatans	chooses
charles	choosing
charm	choral
charmed	chorus
charming	choruses
charms	chose
charred	chosen
chase	christian
chasm	christians
chasms	chronicle
checked	chronology
cheek	chronometers
cheeks	chuckle
cheerful	cigar
cheerfully	cinder
cherish	cinders
chess	circle
chief	circlet
chiefdom	circuitous
chiefly	circular
chiefs	circulates
child	circulation
childhood	circumstance
childish	circumstances
childless	cistern
childlike	cite
children	cities
chill	citizen
chime	citizens
chin	city
chinese	civil
chink	civilisation

civilised

civilities

claim

claimed

clairvoyance

clamber

clambered

clamps

clasp

class

classes

classic

classical

classification

classified

claws

clear

clearance

cleared

clearing

clearly

clearness

cleave

cleaving

cleft

climate

climbing

cling

clinging

clocks

close

closed

closely

closes

closest

clothes

clothing

clouds

cloven

clue

clumsy

clustering

clusters

cogent

coil

coinage

coins

cold

collect

collected

collection

collectively

college

colloquially

colonies

colossal

colour

coloured

colouring

colours

columns

combativeness

combine

combined

combustion

come

comedy

comer

comes

comfort

comforter

comforts

coming

command

commanded

commands

commence

commenced

commencement

commences

commencing

commended

commentators

commerce

commercial

commiseration

commission

commissioned

commissioner

committed

common

commonly

commonplace

commonwealth

commonwealths

communicate

communicated

communication

communications

communities

community

compact

companion

companions

companionship

company

comparable

comparative

comparatively

compare

compared

comparison

compartments

compass

compassion

compassionate

compatriots

compel

compelled

compensation

compete

competence

competent

competition

complacent

complaint

complaisance

complete

completed

completely

completing

complex

complexion

complexions

compliance

complicated

complication

compliment

complimentary

complimented

compliments

compose

composed

composer

composition

compound

compounds

comprehend

comprehended

comprehending

comprehends

compressed

compression

comprise

comprised

comprises

comprising

compunction

computation

compute

conceal

concealed

concealing

conceals

conceded

conceding

conceive

conceives

conceiving

concentrates

concentred

conception

concern

concerned

concerns

concert

concession

conchology

conciliatory

conclude

concluded

conclusions

concomitantly

concur

concurrent

condemn

condescend

condition

conditions

conduce

conduced

conducing

conduct

conducted

conductor

conductors

confer

conferred

confess

confessed

confidant

confide

confidence

confides

confiding

confine

confined

confirm

confirmed

conflict

conformation

conforming

confused

confusedly

confusion

congenial

congress

coniferous

conjecture

conjectured

conjecturing

conjugal

conjugation

connected

connecting

connection

connects

conquer
conqueror
conquerors
conquests
conscience
conscientiousness
conscious
consciousness
consent
consents
consequence
consequences
consequently
conservation
conservatories
consider
considerable
considerably
considerate
consideration
considered
considering
consigned
consist
consisted
consists
consolation
consolations
consorts
conspicuous
constant
constantly
constituent
constitute
constituted
constitutes

constituting

constitution
constitutional
constitutions
constrain
construct
constructed
constructing
construction
construed
consulting
consults
consumed
contact
contain
contained
containing
contains
contemplated
contemplation
contemporaneous
contempt
contemptuous
contend
contended
content
contented
contention
contentions
contentious
contentment
contest
contested
continent
continuance
continue
continued
continues
continuing

continuous
contour
contradict
contradiction
contrary
contrast
contribute
contributed
contrivance
contrivances
contrive
contrived
contrives
control
controlled
controversy
controvert
contusions
convenient
conventions
conversation
converse
conversed
conversing
convertible
convey

conveyances
conveyed
conveying
convict
conviction
convince
convoy
convulsion
convulsions
cookery
coolness

cools
copse
copy
coquette
cord
cordially
corinthian
corn
coronet
corps
corpse
corpuscular
correlation
correlative
correspondent
corresponding
corresponds
corridor
corridors
corrugated
corruption
cost
cotton
couch
could
council
councillors
counsel
counted
countenance
countenances
counteractions
countless
countries
country
countrymen
couple
coupled

courage	creatures
course	credit
court	credulity
courted	credulous
courteous	creed
courteously	creeping
courting	crept
courts	crest
courtship	cried
cover	cries
covered	crime
covering	crimes
coverings	criminal
covers	cringing
covert	critic
covet	critics
covets	crocodile
cowering	crops
cows	crossing
coy	crotchet
craft	crowd
crag	crowded
craggy	crowds
cranach	crown
cranial	crowned
cranium	crowning
cranny	crude
craven	cruel
crawling	cruelty
crazy	crumbled
create	crumbling
	crust
created	cry
creates	crystal
creating	cultivate
creation	cultivated
creator	cultivation
creature	cultivators

culture	darting
cunning	dashed
cup	dat
cupidity	date
curbed	dates
curbing	dative
cure	daubs
curiosities	daughter
curiosity	daughters
curious	day
currency	days
current	dazzled
currents	dazzling
curtain	de
curtained	dead
curtains	deadly
curtly	deal
curved	dealt
cushions	dear
custom	dearer
customer	death
customs	debases
cut	debasing
cwm	debating
cylinders	decaying
daily	decease
dainty	deceased
dance	deceived
dances	decide
danger	decided
dangerous	decides
dangers	declare
dappled	declared
dared	declension
daring	decline
dark	declined
darkness	decoy
darling	decoyed

decreed
deed
deem
deemed
deep
deeper
deeply
deer
defeated
defect
defend
defensive
defer
deference
deferential
defiance
deficient
defied
defiles
define
defined
deformed
defrayed
degenerates
degeneration
degradation
degrade
degraded
degree
degrees
deign
deigned
deity
dejection
deliberating
deliberation
delicacy
delicate

delicately
delicious
delight
delighted
delivering
deluge
demand
demands
demeanour
demi
demigod
democracies
democracy
democratic
demon
demons
demonstrate
demonstration
demosthenes
demure
demurred
den
denied
denominate
denomination
denote
denotes
denoting
deny
depart
departed
department
departments
departure
departures
depend
depended
dependent

depends
depicting
depicts
deporting
deposited
deposits
deprecate
depredation
deprived
depth
depths
deputation
deputed
descartes
descend
descendant
descendants
descended
descending
descent
describe
described
description
desert
deserted
deserts
deserve
deserved
design
designated
designs
desire
desired
desires
desiring
desolate
despair
despatched

despise
despised
despite
despotic
despots
destination
destined
destiny
destitute
destitution
destroy
destroyed
destroyer
destroyers
destroying
destroys
destruction
destructive
destructiveness
desultory
detached
detail
details
detect
detected
deter
deterioration
determination
determine
determined
detestable
devastation
develop
developed
developing
development
develops
devoid

devote

devoted

devoting

devotion

devotions

devour

devoured

devourers

devouring

devoutly

dexterity

diadem

diagonally

dialects

diamond

dictated

dictionary

did

die

died

dies

diet

differ

differed

difference

differences

different

differently

differing

differs

difficult

difficulty

diffused

diffusing

digits

dignified

dignifies

dignitary

dignity

dikes

dilated

dilemma

diligently

diluted

dim

dimensions

diminished

diminutive

dint

direct

directed

direction

directly

disadvantage

disagreeable

disappear

disappeared

disappointed

discharge

discharged

disciple

disciples

discipline

disciplined

disclaiming

discoloration

discontents

discountenance

discourage

discouraged

discouragements

discourteous

discover

discovered

discoverers

discovery

discreetly
discrimination
discussed
discussing
discussion
disdain
disease
diseased
diseases
disentangled
disgraced
disguise
disgust
dishes
dishonourable
disinterested
dislike
dismal

dismayed
dismiss
dismissed
disobeying
disparage
disparagement
disparities
disparity
dispel
dispensed
disperse
dispersed
displaced
displayed
displease
displeased
displeasing
displeasure
disposition

disputants
disputations
dispute
disputes
disputing
disqualified
disregard
disrespectful
dissatisfied
dissect
dissected
dissecting
dissection
dissimilar
dissimulation
dissolution
distance
distances
distant
distinct
distinction
distinctions
distinctly
distinguish
distinguished
distinguishes
distinguishing
distress
distributed
district
districts
distrust
disturbed
disturbing
disuse
diva
divan
divans

diversified

diversions

divert

diverted

diverting

divest

divide

divided

divine

divined

divinity

division

divisions

divorce

divorced

divorces

do

docile

doctrine

does

dog

dogma

dogs

doing

dolichocephalic

dollar

dollars

domain

domains

dome

domestic

dominant

dominion

dominions

don

donation

done

donned

doom

doomed

door

doorless

doors

doorway

doorways

dormant

dost

dotage

double

doubles

doubt

doubtful

doubtless

douches

dove

doves

down

downcast

downwards

dozen

dr

drafted

dramas

draw

drawing

drawings

drawn

draws

dread

dreaded

dreadest

dream

dreamed

dreamers

dreamily

dreaming

dreams	dwelt
dress	dyed
dressed	dying
drew	e
drink	each
drinker	eager
drinks	eagerly
drivelling	eagle
driven	ear
drooped	earlier
dropped	earliest
dropping	early
drowsy	earnest
dry	ears
dual	earth
dubitant	ease
duchess	easily
ductile	eastern
due	easy
duets	eating
dull	eclipsed
duller	edifice
dulness	edifices
dumb	educated
dumbfounded	education
duodecimos	edward
durable	effect
duration	effected
	effects
during	effectually
durst	efficiency
dust	effigies
duties	efflorescence
duty	effort
dwell	efforts
dwelling	effulgence
dwellings	effusions
dwells	egyptian

ei	embittered
eight	embraced
either	emerge
ek	emerged
elaborate	emerging
elaborately	emigrants
elapse	emigrate
elder	emigrated
elderly	emigration
eldest	eminence
elect	eminences
elected	eminent
electric	eminently
electricity	emit
electro	emitted
electrobiology	emotional
elegant	emotions
element	emperor
elements	emphatically
elevated	empire
elevates	employ
elevating	employed
eliminated	employing
elimination	employment
elk	employments
elks	employs
eloquent	empty
else	emulation
elsewhere	emulators
emanate	enable
emanated	enabled
emanates	enabling
embank	enclose
embarrassed	enclosures
embarrassment	encounter
embattled	encountered
embedded	encourage
embers	encouraged

encroachments
end
endearing
endearingly
endeavoured
endeavouring
endeavours
ended
endow
endowed
endowments
ends
endurable

enemies
enemy
energetic
energic
energies
energy
enforce
engaged
engender
engendered
engine
engineer
engines
england
english
englishman
engraven
engulf
enjoy
enjoyable
enjoyed
enjoyment
enjoys
enlarge

enlightened
enlivens
ennui
enormous
enough
enter
entered
entering
enterprise
enters
entertain
entertained
entertainers
entertainment
entertainments
entertains
enthusiasm
enthusiasts
entice
enticed
entire
entirely
entomology
entrails
entrance
entreat
entrusted
enveloped
envied
enviously
envy
epithet
epoch
equable
equal
equality
equally
equals

equilibrium	even
equivalent	event
equivalents	events
erase	ever
ere	every
erring	everything
erroneous	evidence
erudite	evidences
ery	evident
escape	evidently
escaped	evil
escaping	evils
esculent	evince
especial	evinced
especially	evolutions
essay	exact
essence	exacted
essential	exactly
establish	exaggerated
established	exalt
establishes	exalted
estate	exalting
esteems	examination
estimate	examine
estimation	examined
et	examining
etc	example
eternal	examples
eternally	exceeded
eternity	exceedingly
ethereal	exceeds
etruscan	excel
europe	excellence
european	excellences
evade	excelling
evaded	excels
evaporated	except
evasive	exception

exceptions	expense
excess	expensive
excessive	experience
exchange	experiment
exchanged	experimentalist
excite	experiments
excited	expires
excitement	explain
exciting	explained
exclaimed	explanation
exclamation	explanatory
excluded	exploded
excrement	explorations
excursions	explore
excuse	exploring
executed	expose
executioner	exposed
exemption	exposes
exercise	exposing
exercises	express
exhausted	expressed
exhibit	expressing
exhibited	expression
exhibits	expressions
exhilarating	expressive
exist	expressly
existed	exquisite
existence	exquisitely
existent	extant
existing	extend
exists	extended
exorcism	extending
expanded	extends
expanse	extensive
expatiate	extent
expect	exterminate
expecting	exterminated
expedition	extermination

extinct
extinction
extinguished
extirpating
extract
extracted
extracting
extraordinary
extreme
extremely
extrication
eye
eyelids
eyes
fable
fabled
fables

face
faces
fact
factory
facts
faculties
faculty
fade
faded
fades
fail
failed
failing
fails
failure
faint
faintly
faintness
fair
fairer

fairly
faith
faithful
fall
fallen
falling
false
falsehood
falsehoods
falter
faltered
faltering
fame
familiar
familiarity
familiarly
families
family
fanatical
fanaticism
fancied
fanciful
fancy
fangs
fantastic
fantastical
fantastically
far
faraday
farcical
farewell
farming
farms
farther
fascinated
fashion
fashionable
fast

fasten
fastened
fastenings
fastest
fastidious
fatal
fated
father
fatigue
fault
faultless
faults
favour
favourable
favoured
favourite
favours
fear
feared
fearless
fears
feathers
feathery
feats
feature
features
feeble
feeds
feel
feeling
feelingly
feels
feet
felicitous
felicity
fell
felled
fellow

fellows
felt
female
females
feminine
fern
ferns
ferocious
ferocity
fertility
fervently
festival
festivities
festivity
fetter
fever
feverish
few
fibre
fibres
fibrous
fickle
fiction
fie
field
fields
fiends
fierce
fifteen
fifty
fight
figure
figures
filled
fills
final
finally
finches

find
finding
finds
fine
finer
finger
fingers
finite
fire
fires
firm
firmly
first
firstly
fish
fishes
fissure
fist
fit
fits
fitted
five
fix
fixed
fixes
fixing
fixity
flag
flame
flanks
flap
flash
flask
flat
flattering
flavour
flavoured
fled

fleece
flesh
flew
flight
flights
flint
float
floating
flood
floor
flooring
flourish
flourished
flourishes
flowed
flower
flowering
flowers
flown
flows
flue
fluency
fluid
flung
flutterings
fly
flying
folded
foliage
folks
follies
follow
followed
following
follows
folly
fond
fondness

food

fools

foot

footed

footing

footsteps

for

forbade

forbid

forbidden

forbids

force

forced

forces

fore

forefathers

forefinger

foregoes

forehead

foreheads

foreign

foremost

forenoon

foresaw

foresee

foresees

forest

forewarnings

forget

forgot

forgotten

fork

form

formally

formation

formations

formed

former

formerly

formidable

formidably

forming

formless

forms

forsook

forsooth

forth

fortress

fortunately

fortune

forward

fossil

fought

found

foundations

fountain

four

fourth

fragment

fragments

fragrance

fragrant

frame

france

frank

frankly

frankness

free

freed

freedom

freely

french

frequent

frequently

freshness

friend

friendly	g
friends	gaiety
friendship	gain
fright	gained
frivolous	gainers
fro	
frog	gains
froglet	gallant
frogs	gallantry
from	galleries
frontal	gallery
fronted	galvanism
fronting	game
fruit	games
fruitage	garb
fruits	garden
fugitive	gardens
fugitives	garment
fulfil	garments
fulfilled	gas
fulfilment	gases
full	gastric
fullest	gather
fully	gathered
fund	gave
funds	gayest
funeral	gaze
fungi	gazed
funnel	gazing
furnish	gems
furnished	genera
furrow	general
furrows	generality
further	generally
furtively	generals
fusion	generation
futile	generations
future	generosity

genii

genitive

genius

gentle

gentlemen

gentlest

gently

genuine

genuinely

genus

geological

geologists

geology

germanic

gesticulation

gesture

gestures

get

getting

ghastly

ghost

ghosts

giant

giants

giddiest

gift

gifted

gifts

gigantic

girls

give

given

giver

gives

giving

gl

glad

gladdened

glance

glanced

glances

glaring

glass

glata

glaubs

glaubsila

glauran

glazed

gleam

gleamed

gleaming

glek

glide

glided

gliding

glimmered

glimmering

glimpse

globe

gloom

gloomier

gloomy

gloon

glorious

glory

glowing

glowingly

gnomes

go

goad

goal

goat

goats

god

godlike

gods

goes
gold
golden
gone
good
goodness
gorilla
got
gothic
governed
government
governors
grace
graceful
grade
grades
gradual
gradually
grains
graminivorous
grammar
grammarians
grand
grander
grandeur
grandeurs
grandfather
grandmother
grandson
granite
grant
granted
grapes
grappling
grasp
grasps
gratification
gratify

gratifying
gratitude
grave
gravely
graver
gravest
gravity
graze
great
greater
greatest
greatly
greatness
greek
greeks
green
greeting
gregarious
grew
grey
grief
grieve
grieves
grim
groan
grope
groping
gross
ground
groundwork
group
grouped
groups
groves
grown
grows
growth
grudge

grumbled

grumbler

guarantees

guard

guardian

guest

guests

guidance

guide

guided

guiding

guilt

guilty

gulfs

gum

gushed

guy

gy

gymnastic

gyrations

habiliments

habit

habitable

habitation

habitations

habits

habitual

habitually

habituated

had

hair

hairless

hairs

hairy

half

hall

halls

hallucinations

halo

halted

halves

hamlets

hand

handed

handful

handicrafts

handiwork

handle

hands

handsome

handsomest

handwriting

handy

hanging

hannibal

happened

happening

happens

happier

happiest

happily

happiness

happy

hard

harder

hardy

harlot

harm

harmless

harmonies

harmonise

harmony

has

hast

hastened

hastily

hate
have
having
hazard
hazardous
haze
he
head
heads
heal
healer
healing
heals
health
healthful
healthier
heap
heaped
hear
heard
hearing
heart
heat
heated
heathen
heaven
heavenly
heavens
heavenward
heaving
heavy
heels
height
heights
held
helm
help
helped

hemisphere
hence
her

herbage
herbs
here
hereafter
hereditarily
hereditary
herewith
hero
heroic
hers
herself
hesitate
hesitated
hesitates
heterogeneous
hewn
hide
hideous
hiding
hieroglyph
hieroglyphic
high
higher
highest
highly
highness
hil
hilarity

hill
him
himself
hind
hinder

hindrance
hints
hirsute
his
hiss
hissing
historical
history
hither
hitherto
hoarded
hobbies
hold
holding
hole
holes
hollow
hollowed
hollowness
hollows
holmes
holy
homage
home
homely
homes
homeward
honey
honeymoon
honour
honourable
honoured
honours
hooks
hoop
hope
hopeful
hopelessly

hopes
hoping
horizon
horns
horrible
horror
horse
horses
hospitably
hospitality
host
hostile
hot
hotels
hour
hours
house
household
households
houses
hovered
how
however
howsoever
hue
hues
huge
hum
human
humane
humanely
humanity
humble
humbled
humbler
humblest
humid
humiliating

humiliation	ignorant
humour	ii
humours	iii
hundred	ill
hung	illegal
hungarian	illicit
hungrily	illness
hungry	illuminates
hunt	illumine
hunted	illumined
hurried	illustrate
husband	illustrations
husbandry	illustrious
husbands	image
hush	images
hushed	imagination
hut	imaginative
huts	imagine
hymn	imagined
hypocrisy	imitate
i	imitated
ice	imitating
idea	imitations
ideal	immaterial
ideality	immeasurably
ideals	immediate
ideas	immediately
identical	immemorial
identity	immense
idiom	imminent
idiomatic	immodest
idiosyncrasies	immolating
idiotic	immorality
idle	immortal
idly	immortality
if	immortals
ignoble	impartial
ignorance	impartially

impassable
impassioned
impel
impelled
imperceptible
imperfect
imperfectness
imperious
implanted
implements
implicit
implied
implies
implore
imply
implying
importance
important
imported
importunity
impossible
impostures
impregnated
impressed
impression
improper
impropriety
improve
improved
improvement
improvements
impudence
impulse
impurity
in
inability
inanimate
inasmuch

inattentive
inborn
incalculable
incautious
incentive
incentives
inch
inches
incident
incidentally
inclination
inclinations
inclined
inclining
including
incoherent
incommodiously
incompatible
inconceivable
incorrigibly
increase
increased
increases
increasing
incredibly
incredulous
inculcate
inculcates
incumbrances
indecorum
indeed
indefinable
indefinite
independence
independent
independently
indescribable
indestructible

indian

indians

indicate

indicated

indicates

indifference

indifferent

indignantly

indignation

individual

individuals

indo

indolent

indrawn

induce

induced

inducement

indulge

indulged

indulgence

indulgent

indulgently

industries

industry

ineffable

inequalities

inert

inevitable

infancy

infant

infants

infatuation

infected

inferior

infers

infinite

infinitely

infirmities

infirmity

inflammable

inflated

inflectional

inflexible

inflicted

influence

influences

inform

information

informed

infringe

infringed

infused

ingenious

ingenuity

ingenuous

inhabitants

inhabited

inherent

inherit

inheritance

inimical

inimitable

initial

injunction

injuring

injury

injustice

inmate

innate

inner

innocent

innumerable

inoperative

inquired

inquiries

inquiry
inquisitive
inquisitively
insatiable
inscribed
inscrutable
insect
insects
insensible
inseparable
insignia
insignificance
insignificant
insinuate
insipid
insisting
insoluble
inspected
inspecting
inspectors
inspired
inspirer
inspiring
instance
instances
instant
instantly
instead
instinct
instinctive
instinctively
instincts
institute
institutions
instruction
instructress
instrument
instruments

insufficient
insure
insures
intellect
intellectual
intelligence
intelligent
intended
intensity
intently
inter
interchange
interchanged
intercommunicating
intercourse
interdicted
interest
interested
interesting
interests
interfere
interfered
interference
interior
intermarriage
intermarriages
intermarried
intermediate
interment
intermixture
internal
interposed
interrogator
interrogatories
interrupt
interrupted
interspersed
interstices

interval

intervals

intervene

intervening

intervention

interweaving

intestines

intimate

intimates

into

intolerable

intonation

intoxicating

intoxication

introduce

introduced

introduction

intuition

intuitively

inundations

invade

invaded

invaders

invariable

invariably

invasion

invasions

invented

invention

inventions

inventive

inventor

inverted

invest

invested

invests

invigorate

invigorating

invisible

invitations

invite

invited

involve

involved

involves

inward

iron

irony

irreclaimably

irregular

irregularities

irremediable

irreverent

irritated

irruptions

is

isles

isolating

isolation

it

italian

italy

item

its

itself

iv

iva

ix

jackson

jagged

jaw

jaws

jealous

jealousy

jest

jewel

jewels	kindred
join	kinds
joined	king
joining	kings
joins	kinsfolk
journey	kinsman
journeys	kissed
joy	kneading
joyfully	knee
joyous	kneeling
joys	knees
judge	knelt
judged	knew
judges	knife
judgment	know
juice	knowledge
juices	known
jump	knows
jurisprudists	koom
just	krek
justice	labial
justify	labour
juts	labourer
jy	labourers
keen	labouring
keener	labours
keep	labyrinths
keeping	lack
ken	ladies
kept	lady
key	lai
keys	laid
kill	lake
killed	lakes
kills	lambent
kind	lamentable
kindly	lamp
kindness	lamplight

lamplit
lamps
lancinating
land
landed
landmarks
lands
landscape
landscapes
language
languages
languishes
larder
large
largely
largeness
larger
largest
last
lasted
lastingly
lastly
late
lately
latent
later
latest
latter
laugh
laughed
laughter
launched
launching
lavender
lavish
lavished
law
laws

lawyers
lay
laying
lays
lazy
lead
leaden
leading
leads
leaf
leafage
league
leap
learn
learned
learning
learns
least
leave
leaves
leaving
lecture
led
ledge
ledges
left
legend
legends
leggings
legions
legs
leisure
length
lengthened
lengthy
lenient
lent
less

lesser
lessons
lest
let
letter
letters
level
levelled
lewins
liberty
libraries
library
lichen
lid
lie
lies
life
lifeless
lifelike
lift
lifted
lifts
light
lighted
lightened
lighting
lightly
lightning
lightnings
lights
like
liked
likely
likes
liking
limbs
limit
limited

limits
limned
lin
line
lines
linger
lining
link
linked
linnets
lips
liquid
liquids
listen
listened
listener
listeners
listening
lit

literally
literary
literature
little
littleness
live
lived
livelier
lively
liverpool
lives
living
ller
lo
loader
loathsomeness
localities
locked

lodged	lower
lodging	lowered
loftier	lowliest
lofty	luckily
london	lucrative
long	lumber
longed	luminous
longer	lurking
longest	lustre
longevity	lustreless
look	lustrous
looked	luxuries
looking	luxurious
looks	luxury
loomed	lyell
loops	lying
loose	lytton
loosely	m
lore	machine
lose	machinery
losers	machines
loses	made
loss	magical
lost	magistrate
lot	magnetism
lots	magnificent
loud	maid
loudness	maiden
louis	main
love	maintain
loved	maintained
loveliest	maintaining
lovely	maintenance
lover	majestic
lovers	majesty
loves	majority
loving	make
low	maker

makes
making
makings
maladies
male
males
malformation
mammalia
man
management
manganese
manifest
manifestations
manifold
manipulator
mankind
manlike
manly
manner
manners
mantle
mantling
manufactured
many
mar
march
margin
mark
marked
marking
marks
marriage
marriageable
married
marry
marrying
mars
marshalled

martin
marvelled
marvelling
marvellous
marvellously
mass
massacre
masses
massive
massiveness
master
masterpieces
masters
mate
material
materials
mates
mathematical
matlike
matter
matters
matting
mature
matured
max
maxim
maxims
may
me
meagre
meal
meals
mean
meaner
meanest
means
meant
meanwhile

measured
meat
mechanical
mechanician
mechanicians
mechanics
mechanism
medical
medicinal
medicine
meditations
meditative
medium
meet
melancholy
melodious
melody
melt
melted
member
members
membrane
memory
men
menace
menacing
mental
mention
mentioned
mephitic
mercantile
merchandise
merciful
mercifully
mercy
mere
merely
merit

merits
merry
mesmeric
mesmerism
messenger
met
metal
metallic
metals
metaphor
metaphorically
metaphysical
metempsychosis
methought
middle
midst
midway
might
mightiest
mighty
migrate
migrated
mild
mildest
mildly
mildness
miles
military
militate
milk
milking
million
millions
mimics
mind
minds
mine
mineral

minerals	moderate
miners	modern
mines	modes
mingled	modest
minister	modestly
minor	modesty
minute	modified
minutes	modulated
minutest	moli
mirth	moment
mirthful	momentary
misapprehended	moments
misbecome	monarch
misbecomes	monarchies
mischievous	money
miserable	monkey
miseries	monosyllable
misery	monosyllables
misfortune	monotonous
miss	monotony
misshapen	monroe
mission	monster
mistake	monsters
mistaken	monstrous
mistress	montgolfier
misunderstand	month
misuse	months
mitigate	moral
mix	moralising
mixed	moralists
mixture	morality
mmer	morasses
mock	more
mockingly	moreover
mode	morning
model	morrow
modelled	mortal
models	mortals

mortified
most
mostly
mother
mothers
motion
motioned
motionless
motions
motive
motives
mountain
mountains
mounted
mounting
mourners
moustache
mouth
mouths
movable
moved
movement
movements
moving
mr
mrs
much
muddy
multiply
multitude
mummy
murder
murderess
murderous
murmured
murmuring
muscle
muscles

muscular
museum
museums
music
musical
musicians
musing
musingly
must
muttered
mutually
my
myriad
myriads
myself
mysteries
mysterious
mystic
mystical
mystics
mythical
mythology
myths
n
na
nak
naked
name
nameless
names
nan
naphtha
naria
narl
narrated
narrative
narrow
nas

nasal	nerves
nation	nervous
national	nether
nations	nettled
native	neutral
natural	never
	nevermore
naturalist	nevertheless
naturalists	new
naturally	newspapers
nature	newton
naughty	next
nax	nicely
nay	nicest
near	nicety
nearer	night
nearest	nights
nearly	nimbly
necessarily	no
necessary	noah
necessitated	nobility
necessitates	noble
necessities	nobleman
necessity	nobler
neck	noblest
need	nodded
needed	noiselessly
needing	nom
needs	nomenclature
neglected	nominal
negroes	nominally
neighbour	nominative
neighbourhood	none
neighbouring	nonsense
neighbours	noon
neither	noose
nephew	nor
nerve	normal

north
northern
not
notably
notation
note
notes
nothing
notice
noticed
notion
notions
notwithstanding
noun
nouns
novel
novelists

novelties
novelty
now
nowadays
number
numberless
numbers
numerous
nuptial
nurse
nurses
nutritious
o
obedience
obey
obeyed
obeying
obeys
object
objects

obligation
obligations
obliged
obnoxious
obscured
obsequies
observant
observation
observe
observed
observer
observing
obsolete
obstacles
obstruction
obtain
obtained
obtaining
obtains
obtrusive
obvious
obviously
occasion
occasional
occasioned
occasions
occult
occupation
occupations
occupied
occupies
occur
occurred
ocean
odds
odic
odour
of

off	openings
offence	opera
offend	operate
offended	operated
offender	operation
offending	operations
offensive	opinion
offer	opinions
offered	opportunity
office	opposed
officer	opposite
offices	oppress
official	oppressive
offspring	option
often	opulent
oh	or
oils	orange
old	orators
older	orbs
oldest	ordained
olive	order
ological	ordered
ology	orders
omission	ordinarily
omit	ordinary
on	organ
once	organic
one	organisation
	organisations
ones	organised
only	organism
onward	organized
oon	organs
oozes	oriental
opals	orientals
open	origin
opened	original
opening	originally

originate	pace
originated	paces
originating	pack
ornament	paddles
ornamental	pages
ornamented	pah
other	paid
others	pain
otherwise	pained
ought	painfully
our	painless
ours	pains
ourselves	painstaking
out	painted
outbreaks	painter
outlets	painters
outline	painting
outlines	paintings
outrageously	pairs
outraging	palace
outspread	palatable
over	pale
overcharged	palm
overcome	panel
overheard	pang
overhearing	panic
overtasked	paper
overtures	paradise
owed	paramount
owen	paraphrase
owing	parasite
own	parasitical
owned	parcel
owner	pardon
owning	parent
oxygen	parents
oyster	paris
p	parisian

part
partaking
parted
partial
partiality
partially
participation
participators
participle
particle
parties
parting
partly
partner
parts
party
pass
passage
passages
passed
passengers
passers
passes
passing
passion
passionately
passionless
passions
past
pastime
pasture
pastures
pater
patera
path
patiently
patriarchal
patriarchs

patriot
pause
paused
paw
pay
pays
peace
peaceful
peacefully
peal
pear
peculiar
peculiarities
peculiarity
peculiarly
peerless
pellucid
penetrate
penetrated
penury
people
perceive
perceived
perceiving
perceptible
perception
perceptions
perfect
perfected
perfectibility
perfection
perfections
perfectly
perfectness
perform
performed
performers
performs

perfume
perfumed
perfumes
perhaps
peri
peril
perilous
perils
period
periodical
periods
periphrastic
perish
perished
perishes
perishing
permanence
permanency
permeated
permeating

permission
permit
permits
permitted
peroration
perpendicular
perpetual
perpetually
perpetuity
perplexed
perplexes
persecuted
persecution
perseverance
persevered
person
personage

personages
personal
persons
perspective
persuaded
persuading
persuasion
persuasions
persuasive
pervade
pet
petre
petroleum
pets
petty
petulance
petulant
phantom
phase
phases
phenomena
phenomenon
philanthropists
philip
philological
philologist
philologists
philoprogenitiveness
philosopher
philosophers
philosophical
philosophically
philosophies
philosophy
phosphorescent
photograph
phrenologist
phrenologists

physical

physically

physician

physicians

picks

pictorial

pictures

picturesque

piece

pieces

piercing

pigments

pillows

pinch

pined

pinions

pioneers

pious

pipe

piping

pistol

pithiness

pithy

pity

place

placed

places

placing

plain

plainly

planet

plant

plants

plaster

plate

plates

platform

platforms

plato

platter

plausibility

play

played

playful

playing

playmates

plays

plaything

pleading

pleasant

please

pleased

pleases

pleasing

pleasurable

pleasure

pledge

pledged

pliant

plies

plinths

ploughshare

plumage

plumes

plunder

plunged

plunging

plural

ply

pocket

poem

poet

poetic

poetical

poetry

poets

point	portrait
pointed	portraits
pointing	portraiture
points	posh
poise	position
poised	positive
poising	possess
police	possessed
policy	possession
polish	possessions
polished	possibility
polite	possible
politely	
politeness	possibly
political	post
politically	posterity
politicians	potent
politics	potential
polity	potently
polygamy	poverty
polysyllabic	powder
polysynthetical	power
pomp	powerful
poo	powerfully
poodle	powerless
pools	powers
poor	pra
poorer	practical
poosh	practice
populace	practices
popular	practise
popularly	practised
population	practitioner
populations	practitioners
porch	praise
pores	pray
porousness	prayed
portion	prayer

prayers
pre
preceded
precedence
precedes
preceding
precepts
precious
precipitated
precipitating
precipitous
precisely
precocious
precociously
predictions
predilection
predilections
predominance
predominant
prefer
preference
preferred
preferring
prefers
prefix
prehistorical
prejudices
premature
prematurely
preoccupied
preparation
prepared
preponderant
preponderate
preposition
prepositions
presence
present

presented
presenting
presently
presents
preservation
preserve
preserved
preserving
presiding
pressed
pressing
pressure
presume
presumed
pretend
pretends
preterite
prettily
prettiness
prettinesses
pretty
prevail
prevailed
prevailing
prevails
prevalent
prevent
prevented
previous
previously
prey
price
prices

prickly
pride
primary
primeval

primitive	profligate
princess	profound
principal	profuse
principally	progenitors
principle	progress
principles	progressive
private	project
privilege	projectile
privileged	projection
prize	projections
probability	projects
probable	prolonged
probably	promenades
probation	prometheus
problem	prominent
problems	promise
proceed	promises
proceeded	promotion
proceeds	prompt
process	prompts
proclaiming	pronounced
produce	pronounces
produced	pronunciation
produces	proof
producing	properly
product	properties
production	property
productive	prophetically
products	proportion
profess	proportionate
professed	proportionately
professional	proportioned
professions	proportions
professor	proposal
professors	propose
proficiency	proposed
proficient	proposing
profit	propre

proprietor
proscribed
prospective
protect
protecting
protection
protective
protector
protruded
proud
prove
proved
proverb
proverbial
proverbs
proves
provide
provided
providence
providing
provision
provoke
provoking
prudish
puberty
public
publications
pugnacious
pulling
pulls
punish
punishments
pupil
pur
pure
purely
purest
purifying

purple
purport
purpose
purposely

purposes
pursue
pursued
pursues
pursuit
pursuits
pushed
put
puts
pyramid
pyramidal
pyramids
quagmire
qualifications
qualities
quality
quarrel
quarrelsome
quarter
quartettes
question
questioned
questionings
questions
quicken
quickened
quickens
quicker
quickly
quiet
quietly
quietude
quit

quite
quitted
quitting
rabbit
race
races
racked
radiance
radiant
radical
raged
railway
raised
raising
rally
rallying
ran
rang
range
ranged
ranges
rank
ranked
ranks
rapid
rapidity
rapidly
rapport
rapt
rare
rarely
rash
rate
rather
ratio
ratiocination
rational
ravage

ravages
ravines
raw
ray
rays
re
reach
reached
reaching
reaction
read
reader
readers
readier
readily
reading
reads
ready
real
realise
realising
reality
really
realm
realms
reaping
reappeared
rear
reared
rearing
reason
reasonable
reasoner
reasoning
reasonings
reasons
rebuilding
recall

recalled
recalling
recede
receding
receive
received
receives
receiving

recent
recently
recess
recesses
reckoning
reclined
reclosed
recognisable
recognise
recognised
recognising
recognition
recoiled
recoiling
recollect
recollected
recollecting
recollection
recollections
recommending
reconcile
reconciled
reconciles
record
recorded
records
recover
recovered
recovering

recreation
red
reddish
reduce
reduced
reduces
reduction
reference
referred
referring
refinement
refining
reflected
reflection
reflections
reflective
reform
reforms
refraining
refreshing
refuge
refuse
refused
refuses
regain
regained
regard
regarded
region
regions
regret
regular
regulate
regulating
regulation
regulations
reign
reject

rejected	remembering
rejects	remembrance
rejoices	reminded
rejoin	remnant
relapse	remorse
related	remote
relates	removed
relation	removing
relations	remuneration
relationship	rend
relative	render
release	rendered
released	rendering
relentlessly	renders
relics	renew
relied	renewed
relief	renounce
relies	renown
relieved	renowned
religion	reopened
religious	repast
religiously	repeat
relinquish	repeated
relinquished	repeating
reluctant	repeats
rely	repel
relying	replace
remain	replenish
remained	replied
remaining	reply
remains	replying
remark	report
remarkable	reports
remarked	repose
remarks	reposes
remedial	represent
remember	representation
remembered	represents

reproach
reproachful
reproachfully
reproduced
reprove
reproving
reptile
reptiles
republic
republican
republics
repugnance
repugnant
repulsive
reputation
repute
request
requested
requesting
requests
require
required
requires
requiring
rescues
research
researches
resemblance
resemble
resembled
resembles
resembling
resents
reserve
reserved
reside
residence
resign

resigned
resist
resisted
resolute
resolutely
resolution
resolve
resolved
resort
resources
respect
respectful
respecting
respects
responsibilities
responsibility
responsible
rest
rested
resting
restless
restored
restrain
restrict
restricted
restriction
rests
result
resulting
results
resumed
retail
retain
retained
retains
retire
retired
retires

retraced	riot
return	rise
returned	risen
returning	rising
reunion	risk
reunite	rival
reunited	rivalry
reveal	rivals
revealed	riven
revenue	rivulet
reverence	rivulets
reverential	road
reverie	roads
reversal	rob
reverse	robert
revisit	robes
revive	rock
revolution	rocks
revolutions	rocky
revolvers	rod
revulsion	roman
rewards	romance
rhythmical	romances
rhythms	roof
rich	roofless
richer	room
riches	rooms
richest	root
richly	rooted
richness	rooting
rid	roots
ridge	rope
ridiculed	ropes
right	rose
rightly	roseate
rights	rot
rigid	rough
ring	roughest

round
rounded
rounder
roundness
roused
rousing
routine
rovings
royal
rudder
rude
rudeness
ruder
rudest
rudiment
rudiments
ruin
ruins
rule
rulers
rules
run
running
runs
rural
rushed
rustic
ruthless
ruthlessly
ruthlessness
s
sabbat
sacred
sad
saddened
safe
safely
safety

sagacity
sage
sages
said
sails
sake
salamanders
salient
salliance
salt
salubrious
salutary
salutation
saluted
samd
same
sana
sandals
sang
sanguine
sank
sanskrit
sar
sat
sate
satire
satisfaction
satisfactory
satisfied
satisfy
sauces
savage
savages
save
saved
saw
saxon
say

sayest	secondly
saying	secret
sayings	secretly
says	sect
scale	section
scaled	sections
scaly	secure
scanty	secured
scarce	securing
scarcely	sedate
scared	seductive
scattered	see
scattering	seeds
scene	seeing
scent	seek
scholars	seeking
school	seeks
schoolboy	seem
schools	seemed
science	seeming
sciences	seemingly
scientific	seems
scientifically	seen
scope	seize
scorn	seized
screened	seldom
scruple	select
scrutiny	selected
sculptured	selecting
sea	selection
search	selects
seasons	self
seat	selfish
seated	sells
seaweeds	semicircle
sec	
second	senate
secondary	senator

sends
sensation
sense
senses
sensible
sensibly
sensitiveness
sent
sentence
sentences
sententious
sentient
sentiment
sentiments
separate
separated
separately
separation
sepulchres
serene
serenity
series
serious
seriously
serpent
serpents
servant
servants
serve
served
serves
service
services
serving
set
sets
settle
settled

settlement
settlements
seven
seventy
several
severance
severed
severer
severest
severing
severity
sex
sexes
sexual
shades
shadow
shadows
shaft
shake
shakespeare
shall
shallow
shalt
shame
shameful
shape
shaped
shapes
shaping
share
shared
shares
sharpen
shatter
shattered
she
shearing
shed

sheds	shrinking
sheep	shrubs
sheer	shrunk
sheets	shudder
shelf	shuddered
shell	shun
shelter	shut
shelves	shutter
sheridan	shy
shifting	si
shining	sibilant
ship	sick
shivered	sickly
shoals	side
shock	sided
shocked	sidelong
shone	sides
shook	sidney
shop	sigh
shopkeeper	sighed
shops	sighing
short	sight
shortened	sign
shorter	signal
shortly	signalised
shot	signally
should	significant
shoulder	signification
shoulders	significations
shouldst	signify
show	signifying
showed	signs
showered	sila
showing	silence
shown	silent
shows	silently
shrank	silly
shrewdness	silvery

similar	skin
simoom	skirting
simple	skull
simpler	sky
simplest	slanders
simplicity	slang
simplified	slanting
simply	slate
sin	slaughter
since	slay
sinews	sleek
sinful	sleep
sing	slender
singing	slenderness
single	slept
singling	slew
sings	slide
singular	slided
singularly	slides
sinking	sliding
sinning	slight
sins	slightest
sir	slightly
sister	sloped
sisters	slow
sit	slowly
sits	slumber
sitting	sly
sittings	small
six	smaller
sixteen	smallest
size	smile
sizes	smiled
sketched	smite
skilfully	smooth
skill	smoothly
skilled	smoothness
skimming	smote

smouldered
smouldering
snort
snuff
so
soar
soared
soaring
soarings
sober
sobriety
soc
social
societies
society
soft
soften
softened
softening
softer
softest
softly
softness
soil
sojourn
sojourned
solace
sold
sole
solely
solemn
solicit
solid
solidity
solitary
solitude
solution
solve

solved
sombre
some
something
sometimes
somewhat
somewhere
son
song
songs
sonorous
sons
soon
soothe
soothing
sorrow
sorrowfully
sorrows
sorry
sort
sough
sought
soul
souls
sound
sounds
source
sources
south
sovereign
sovereignty
sowing
space
spaces
spacious
spare
spared
sparing

sparingly
sparks
spars
spasmodic
speak
speaking
speaks
special
specially
species
specific
specify
specimen
specimens
speck
speculation
speculations
speculative
speech
speechless
speed
speedy
spell
spent
sphere
sphinx
spirit
spirits
spiritual
splash
splendid
splendour
splinters
split
spoke
spoken
sport
sporting

sportive
sportively
sports
spot
spots
spouse
sprang
spray
spread
spreading
spring
springs
spurious
squadrons
square
staff
stag
stage
stages
stairs
stalks
stand
standard
standing
staple
star
stared
starry
stars
started
starting
startled
startling
starts
starved
state
stated
stately

states
station
stationed
stature
status
staves
stay
steadfastly
steadier
steadily
steadiness
steady
steak
stealing
steam
steel
steered
stems
stepped
steps
stern
sternly
sternness
stifle
stigmatised
still
stimulant
stimulants
stimulates
stimulus
stint
stipulated
stir
stirred
stock
stole
stomach
stone

stones
stood
stopped
stops
stored
storehouses
stories
storm
storms
story
stout
stowe
stowed
strain
straining
strand
strange
strangely
strangeness
stranger
strangers
strata
stratification
stratum
streaks
streamed
streams
street
streets
strength
strengthener
stretch
stretched
stricken
stride
strife
strike
striking

strings
stripes
strive
strives
striving
stroked
stroll
strolled
strong
stronger
strongest
strongly
strove
struck

structure
struggle
struggled
struggles
struggling
stubborn
students
studied
studies
study
stuff
stun
stunned
style
styled
suave
subdivide
subdivided
subdued
subject
subjected
subjects
submerged

submissive
submitted
subordinate
subsequently
subservient
substance
substances
subterranean
subtle
subtler
subtlest
succeeded
succeeding
success
successful
successfully
succession
successor
successors
succour
succulent
such
sucked
sudden
suddenly
suffered
suffering
suffers
suffice
sufficed
suffices
sufficient
sufficiently
sufficing
suffix
sugar
suggest
suggested

suggestion	sure
suit	surely
suitable	surest
suited	surface
suitors	surfaces
sum	surgical
summed	surmounted
summer	surpassed
summoned	surpassing
sumner	surplus
sun	surprise
sundry	surprised
sunless	surprising
sunlight	surrender
sunlit	surrounded
super	surrounding
superintending	surveyed
superior	survive
superiority	survived
superseded	surviving
superstitions	survivor
superstitious	susceptibility
superstitiously	susceptible
superterrestrial	suspect
supplant	suspected
supplied	suspend
supplies	suspended
supply	suspending
supplying	suspends
support	suspicion
supported	sustain
supporting	sustained
supports	sustainer
suppose	sustaining
supposed	sustains
supposes	sustenance
supremacy	swan
supreme	sweating

sweep
sweet
sweetness
swift
swifter
swiftly
swimmer
swimming
swollen
swoop
swoops
syllables
symbolical
symbolised
symmetrical
symmetry
sympathetic
sympathising
sympathy
symphonious
synonym
synonymous
system
systematic
systems
t
ta
table
tables
tablet
tablets
tacitly
taciturn
tact
tactics
tadpole
tail
tailor

take
taken
takes
taking
tale
tales

talk
talked
talking
talks
tall
taller
tallest
tamable
tame
tamed
tangle
tapering
tar
tasks
taste
tastes
taught
tax
taxation
teach
teachers
tear
tears
teems
teeth
telegraphic
telegraphs
telescope
tell
tells
temerarious

temper
temperament
temperance
temperate
temperature
temple
temples
temptations
tempted
ten
tenanted
tend
tended
tendency
tender
tenderly
tenderness
tending
tends
tense
term
termed
terminal
terminate
terminating
termination
terminations

terms
terraced
terrestrial
terrible
terribly
territories
territory
terror
tesselated
test

tested
texture
th
than
thank
thanked
thanks
thanksgiving
that
the
theatres
thee
theft
their
theirs
them
theme
themselves
then
thence
theological
theoretical
theories
theory
there
thereby
therefore
therein
thereof
thereon
therewith
these
thews
they
thick
thicker
thin
thine

thing

things

think

thinkers

thinking

thinks

third

thirst

thirty

this

thither

thoroughfare

those

thou

though

thought

thoughtful

thoughts

thousand

thousands

threading

threaten

threatened

three

threshold

thrill

thrilled

thriving

throat

throes

throne

thrones

throngs

through

throughout

throw

throwing

thrown

thumb

thus

thy

thyself

tiara

tie

tiers

tiger

tigers

till

time

timepieces

times

timidity

tint

tired

tis

tish

titian

title

titles

to

toes

together

toil

toiled

toils

token

told

tolerate

tone

tones

tongue

too

took

tools

top

topic

tormented
tortured
tossed
total
touch
touched
touches
touching
tour
towards
towers
town
towns
trace
traced
traces
tract
tracts
trade
trading
tradition
traditional
traditions
traffic
tragedy
trained
training
trains
tramp
trance
trances
tranquil
tranquillity
transactions
transfer
transferred
transfers
transformation

transit
transition
transitions
transitory
translate
transmission
transmit
transmitted
transparent
transpiration
travail
travel
traveller
travellers
travels
traverse
treacherous
treacherously
treasury
treated
treating
tree
trees
tremble
tremblingly
tremor
trial
trials
tribe
tribes
tried
trifle
triflings
trios
trivial
trope
trouble
troubled

troubles
troublesome
true
truly
trust
trusty
truth
truthfulness
try
trying
tubes
tubular
tumbled
tune
tuned
tunes
tunic
tur
turanian
turbulences
turbulent
turkish
turn
turned
turning
turns
tutors
twat
twelve
twenty
twice
twilight
two
type
types
tyrannical
tyranny
u

ugly
ultimate
un
unaccustomed
unacquainted
unalluring
unarmed
unattainable
unattended
unawares
unceasing
uncertain
unchecked
uncivilised
unclosed
uncommon
unconcernedly
unconscious
unconsciously
uncontrollable
uncovered
uncultivated
uncut
under
undergoing
underlying
undermine
understand
understanding
understood
undertake
underwent
undiscovered
undismayed
undistinguished
undisturbed
undulated
undulating

undulous

uneducated

unenlightened

unerring

unerringly

unfamiliar

unfitted

unfortunate

unfurled

unglazed

ungrateful

unguessed

unhallowed

unhappily

unhappy

uniform

uniformly

uninhabitable

uninhabited

unintelligible

union

unite

united

unities

uniting

unity

universal

universe

unjust

unknown

unless

unlike

unlooked

unmarried

unmistakable

unmixed

unmolested

unnoticed

unobserved

unobtrusive

unpenetrated

unpleasant

unpleasing

unquestionably

unreasonable

unreasonably

unreclaimed

unrestrained

unrestricted

unsafe

unsatisfactory

unsound

unspeakable

unstung

untamable

untamably

until

untouched

untrammelled

untranslatable

untruth

unusually

unutterable

unutterably

unwedded

unwelcome

unwillingness

unwise

unwittingly

unworthy

up

uphold

upon

upper

uppermost

upward	variance
urban	variations
urged	varied
urging	variegated
us	varies
use	varieties
used	variety
useful	various
useless	vary
uses	varying
usual	vases
usually	vast
usurped	vastness
utility	vaulted
utmost	vaults
utopian	veed
utter	veedya
utterance	vegetable
uttered	vegetables
uttering	vegetation
utterly	vehemence
uttermost	vehement
v	vehicle
vacancy	vehicles
vague	vehicular
vaguely	veneration
vain	vengeance
valley	venomous
valleys	vent
valour	vents
valuable	venture
value	ventured
valued	verb
van	verbal
vanish	verbs
vanished	verge
vanity	vernal
vapour	verses

vertebrata	visits
very	vista
vessels	vitality
vest	vitiated
vestige	vituperation
veteran	vivacious
vex	vividly
vexed	viz
vi	voc
viands	vocation
vices	vocations
vicinity	vocative
vied	vogue
view	voice
views	voices
vigilant	void
vigorous	volcanic
vigour	volition
vii	volumes
viii	voluntary
vilest	volunteered
vinous	voluptuous
violated	vote
violent	vouch
virgin	vouchsafe
virtually	vouchsafed
virtue	voyages
virtues	vril
virtuous	vulgar
visible	vying
visibly	wafted
vision	waiting
visions	waits
visit	waking
visited	walk
visiting	walked
visitor	walking
visitors	walks

wall	waters
walls	wave
wand	way
wander	ways
wandered	wayside
wanderer	we
wandering	weaker
wanderings	weakness
wanders	wealth
wands	wealthiest
want	wealthy
wanted	weapons
wanting	wear
wanton	wearer
wants	wearied
war	wears
warble	weather
warehouse	weave
warehouses	webbed
warlike	webster
warm	wed
warmer	wedded
warmth	wedding
warn	wedlock
warning	week
warns	weeks
warring	weigh
wars	weight
was	weighty
wash	welcome
washington	welfare
waste	well
watch	wellbeing
watched	welsh
watches	wendel
watching	went
watchmakers	were
water	wert

what	widened
whatever	wider
whatsoever	widow
wheat	widowed
wheels	wielded
when	wife
whence	wild
whenever	wilder
where	wilderness
whereabouts	wilds
whereas	wilfully
wherefore	will
wherein	willing
wherever	willingly
wherewith	willingness
whether	wills
which	wilt
while	win
whims	wind
whimsical	window
whine	windows
whishing	winds
whisky	wines
whisper	wing
whispered	winged
whispers	wings
white	winos
whither	winter
who	wisdom
whoever	wise
whole	wiser
wholesale	wisest
wholly	wish
whom	wishes
whose	wit
why	witches
wide	with
widely	withheld

within
without
witness
witnessed
wits
wives
woe
woke
woman
womanhood
womankind
women
won
wonder
wonderful
wonderfully
wondering
wonderingly
wonders
wont
woo
wooed
wooing
woos
word
words
wore
work
worked
working
works
world
worldly
worlds
worms
worn
worse
worship

worst
worth
would
wouldst
wound
wounded
wranglers
wrangling
wretched
wrinkle
wrist
write
writers
writes
writing
written
wrong
wrote
x
xi
xii
xiii
xiv
xix
xv
xvi
xvii
xviii
xx
xxi
xxii
xxiii
xxiv
xxix
xxv
xxvi
xxvii
xxviii

ya

yam

yan

yani

yards

yawned

year

yearly

yearn

years

yellow

yes

yet

yiam

yield

yoke

yonder

york

you

young

younger

youngest

your

yours

yourself

yourselves

youth

yril

z

zam

zee

zi

zoo

zoologist

zu

zummer

zutze

zuzulia

Printed in Great Britain
by Amazon